WAYLAND

A LOOK AT LIFE IN

The **Nineties**

Judith Condon

This edition published in 2000 by
Wayland Publishers Ltd

First published in 1999 by
Wayland Publishers Ltd,
61 Western Road,
Hove,
East Sussex BN3 1JD

This book was prepared for Wayland Publishers Ltd
by Ruth Nason.

Series editor: Alex Woolf
Series design: Stonecastle Graphics/Carole Design
Book design: Ruth Nason

Cover photographs

Top left: Nelson Mandela, April 1990
(Topham Picturepoint)

Top right: Dolly the Sheep, 25 February
1997 (Popperfoto)

Centre: Brazil's Romario kissing the
FIFA cup, Los Angeles, 17 July 1994
(Popperfoto)

Bottom left: The Spice Girls at the
1996 Smash Hits Poll Winners Party
(Topham Picturepoint)

Bottom right: Rollerblading (Pam
Francis, Robert Harding Picture
Library)

Find Wayland on the internet at:
http://www.wayland.co.uk

British Library Cataloguing in Publication Data

Condon, Judith
  A look at life in the nineties
  1. History, Modern - 20th century - Juvenile
  literature
  2. Nineteen nineties - Juvenile literature
  I. Title II. Nineties
  909.8'29

ISBN 0 7502 2658 7

Printed and bound in Italy by G. Canale & C.S.p.A.,
Turin

Acknowledgements
The Author is grateful to Rosanne and Ewan Flynn
for up-to-the-minute advice on culture and sport.

The Author and Publishers thank the following
for their permission to reproduce photographs:
Camera Press: pages 4-5b, 6b, 7t, 18t, 18b, 19b,
20t, 21l, 24b, 27t, 36b, 37b, 38t, 41; Popperfoto:
pages 4t, 5t, 6t, 7b, 8, 9t, 9b, 10t, 10b, 11t, 11b,
12, 14t, 14b, 15, 16t, 17, 19t, 20b, 21r, 22t, 22b,
23t, 23b, 24t, 25t, 25b, 26, 27b, 28, 29t, 29b, 30,
31t, 31b, 32t, 32b, 33, 34t, 34b, 35, 36-37t, 38b,
40t, 40b; Robert Harding Picture Library: pages
16b (NASA/Phototake NYC), 39 (Pam Francis);
Science Photo Library: pages 13t, 13b.

Quotations are from: page 4: Nelson Mandela,
inauguration address, Pretoria, 10 May 1994;
page 13: Dr Patrick Dixon, *The Genetic Revolution*,
Kingsway Publications, 1993; page 20: *The
Independent*, 30 September 1998; page 23: quoted
in *Chronicle of the Year 1996*, Dorling Kindersley,
1997; page 26: *Antony Gormley*, Phaidon Press,
1995; page 29: the citation of the Stirling Prize for
outstanding architecture, 1998; page 34: Nick Bitel,
on behalf of athlete Dougie Walker, in *The Guardian*,
1 April 1999.

Contents

A Look at...

...in the '90s

A LOOK AT
THE NEWS
IN THE '90s

In 1990 the news seemed hopeful in many ways. The Cold War (long-term hostility between the Western capitalist countries and the communist bloc) had ended. People in the USSR and Eastern Europe were beginning to enjoy new political freedoms. They hoped that economic change would bring a better life.

▷ *Residents of a black township east of Johannesburg queue to vote in South Africa's first all-race elections, April 1994.*

In South Africa, where black people had waged a long struggle for equal rights, against an oppressive white government, the majority of people were looking forward to building a new society, based on justice for all. In 1990, Nelson Mandela and other African National Congress (ANC) leaders were freed from prison. In the country's first general election in 1994, Mandela became president.

On becoming president of South Africa, Nelson Mandela said:

'The time for the healing of wounds has come, the moment to bridge the chasms that divide us has come, the time to build is upon us.'

War in the Gulf

The general optimism did not last long. In the summer of 1990, Iraq, an Islamic country led by dictator Saddam Hussein, invaded Kuwait. The region contained about half the world's reserves of oil and gas, so a great deal was at stake. In January 1991, US, British, French, Egyptian and other forces, acting with United Nations Security Council approval, launched Operation Desert Storm, to remove Iraqi forces from Kuwait. Saddam declared it would be

▷ *As the Iraqis retreated from Kuwait, they set fire to Kuwait's oil wells. Two Kuwaitis survey the damage.*

'the mother of all battles', but could not match the weaponry and power of those ranged against him. Fifty thousand Iraqi soldiers were killed in the war.

Having driven the Iraqis from Kuwait, the allied leaders called a halt. They set up and patrolled 'no-fly zones' around Iraq, to contain Saddam, and hoped the Iraqi people would overthrow him. But he ruthlessly held on to power. In the following years, despite sanctions which isolated Iraq from world trade, UN inspectors found evidence that Saddam was stock-piling nuclear and chemical weapons. NATO planes bombed suspected Iraqi arms factories in 1998, but the dictator remained, and the Iraqi people continued to suffer.

The end of the USSR

Mikhail Gorbachev, leader of the USSR, had helped modernize his country and end the Cold War. But his own people blamed him for the food shortages, uncertainty and loss of world power status that followed. Communist hardliners were also against Gorbachev's efforts to bring more openness and change to the USSR. In August 1991 they tried to seize power. Soldiers held Gorbachev and his wife captive in their holiday villa in Crimea, while tanks moved into Moscow. Boris Yeltsin, the President of Russia, urged people in Moscow to resist the hardliners' coup, and in two days it collapsed. Gorbachev returned, but was soon pushed aside by Yeltsin.

▷ *Moscow, August 1991: Boris Yeltsin urges support for Gorbachev against the hardliners' coup.*

By the end of 1991 the USSR had been dissolved. Some republics had broken away to form independent countries, but others – including Chechnya – remained tied to Russia. In 1994 Yeltsin sent his army to intervene against a separatist uprising in Chechnya. After two years of fighting, with 30,000 lives lost, a treaty was patched together, but Chechnya remained dangerous and unstable.

With the Communist Party out of power in Russia, Yeltsin introduced drastic reforms to the economy, such as lifting state controls on prices. Unemployment, and crime, grew. By 1998 Russia was deep in debt, and the ruble was devalued. People's savings were almost worthless, and many worked without pay for months on end.

Profile

Slobodan Milosevic

Milosevic was a communist leader in Yugoslavia at the end of the 1980s. As communism crumbled, he rallied support for Serbian nationalism and crushed opposition by controlling the army and the media. He resisted independence for the Yugoslav republics, and presided over 'ethnic cleansing'. For years he outmanoeuvred the EC, the USA and the UN, who were reluctant to commit troops to a land war against him. In 1999 NATO bombing forced a Serb withdrawal from Kosovo. Milosevic was charged with war crimes.

Yugoslavia

In 1990 Yugoslavia was a country made up of six republics (Slovenia, Croatia, Bosnia, Serbia, Montenegro and Macedonia) and two provinces (Kosovo and Vojvodina), held together under a communist system formed after the Second World War.

In 1991, Slovenia and Croatia declared independence. Serbian leader Slobodan Milosevic, who controlled the Yugoslav federal army, opposed them. The situation was complex because people of different ethnic backgrounds lived side by side, in different proportions, in each republic. Some people of Serbian origin in Croatia formed paramilitary units, and called on the federal army for support. Milosevic's forces attacked both Croatia and Slovenia. Similar strife spread to Bosnia Herzegovina, where a large Muslim population came under Serb attack.

The nationalism and hatred that had been stirred up led to what was called 'ethnic cleansing' – the forced driving out of local populations, accompanied by appalling cruelty. Ancient cities such as Vukovar in Croatia and Sarajevo in Bosnia were besieged and shelled.

▽ *April 1999: ethnic Albanians, driven from their homes in Kosovo, arrive in Albania.*

▷ In central Africa, in 1994, conflict broke out between the Hutu and Tutsi peoples of Rwanda. Whole villages of Tutsi were massacred (right). Hutus fled the country, fearing retaliation, and vast refugee camps formed. As the decade closed, famine and disease stalked the once green and productive land.

Although the IRA continued a bombing campaign to try to end British rule in Northern Ireland, a slow peace process began, partly inspired by events in South Africa. In 1996, when talks broke down, the IRA detonated huge bombs at Canary Wharf, London, and in Manchester. US Senator George Mitchell helped the Irish and British governments, loyalists, republicans and others to resume their difficult

The European Community (EC) tried to negotiate peace, but numerous ceasefires were broken. In 1994, NATO planes went into offensive action for the first time, against Serb planes, to protect a no-fly zone created by the UN over Bosnia. In 1995 an uneasy peace agreement was signed in Dayton, Ohio. An international force was sent to police the ceasefire in Bosnia. Some leaders of atrocities were declared guilty of war crimes.

negotiations. The Good Friday Agreement was signed in 1998 and, in referendums, people in both Northern Ireland and the Irish Republic voted in favour of it.

In 1998 trouble flared again in the province of Kosovo, where the majority of people were of Albanian origin and supported some form of independence. Serb paramilitaries drove Kosovo Albanians from their homes, turning them into refugees. Thousands were beaten or killed. In March 1999, NATO began air attacks on Serb military targets, to defend Kosovo Albanians. On 9 June, the Serbs surrendered.

A long road to peace
International efforts to broker peace in two long-running conflicts – in Ireland and in the Middle East – saw former enemies at last accepting the need to listen to one another.

△ US President Clinton congratulates Israel's Prime Minister Yitzhak Rabin (left) and Palestine Liberation Organization (PLO) leader Yasser Arafat on the Oslo Accords, 1993. In 1995 Rabin was assassinated by a Jewish extremist opposed to the peace process. The process slowed under the next prime minister, Binyamin Netanyahu. In 1999 he was replaced by Ehud Barak.

A global economy

It became clear that, in several important respects, we all live in one world. International trading and the computerization of banks and stock exchanges meant that money and investment could be moved fast around the world. Some multi-national companies were richer and more powerful than many countries. They concentrated manufacturing in poorer countries, where people would work for lower wages, and so manual workers in other countries found it hard to get jobs.

In the mid-1990s Japan's economy began to falter. Next things started to go wrong in the countries of Southeast Asia (previously called 'tiger' economies, because they had grown so strong, so fast), and in 1998 Russia lurched into economic crisis. Fear grew of worldwide recession, bringing more unemployment and poverty. But the US and European economies remained relatively strong. In 1999, a world-wide campaign called for developing countries to be let off some of their debts to international banks, to boost growth in these countries.

...Newsflash...

Hong Kong, 30 June 1997. On the stroke of midnight, local time, Britain handed Hong Kong over to China, ending more than 150 years of colonial rule. At a ceremony held in torrential rain, governor Chris Patten appealed to China to allow full democratic rights to the people of this booming capitalist city. China currently boasts 'one country, two systems'. Its Special Economic Zones are run on capitalist lines, but the rest of the country is communist. Despite uncertainty about their future, the Chinese population of Hong Kong are celebrating through the night.

International human rights

Native Americans, the Inuit in Canada and the aboriginal people in Australia won greater political rights and recognition of the harm

Profile

Aung San Suu Kyi

In 1988 the people of Burma rose against their military rulers. Aung San Suu Kyi led the pro-democracy movement. As the campaign grew, the generals panicked and arrested her. Still, when elections were held, her National League for Democracy won 82 per cent of the vote. The generals then arrested MPs and killed demonstrators. In 1991 Suu Kyi was awarded the Nobel Peace Prize for her bravery. However, she remained under house arrest all through the 1990s. Crowds gathered at her gate and she spoke out when she could.

◁ *In 1998, 9,000 people were killed when Hurricane Mitch tore through Nicaragua and Honduras, causing floods, mudslides and tidal waves. Roads and bridges, like this one on the main road into Managua, were washed away, making it difficult for relief workers to get through.*

There were floods in the Netherlands, Belgium, northwest Germany and northeast France in 1995. And eastern Germany was devastated in 1997, when the River Oder burst its banks. Bangladesh suffered particularly bad floods in 1991 and 1998.

done when their land was colonized by Europeans. In the 1990s, multi-national companies were likened to the old colonial powers. In Columbia and Brazil they were accused of trampling on human rights and polluting the environment. In Nigeria, oil companies collaborated with a harsh military government to exploit Ogoniland. Ken Saro-Wiwa led local people in protest. When he and eight of his fellows were executed in 1995, there was international outcry.

A global climate

Most of the warmest years of the century were in the 1990s. Man-made chemicals in the atmosphere were blamed for causing global warming, which contributed to a series of record climate events. Mississippi, USA, saw its worst floods ever in 1993, with 20 million acres under water. Parts of Egypt and Italy were deluged in 1994, leaving hundreds dead.

El Niño

Warming in the Pacific Ocean in 1997 (a periodic effect known as 'El Niño') caused problems far away. In Indonesia, El Niño was followed by a drought, made worse by the burning of forests to clear land. For weeks, thick smog covered Borneo, Indonesia and Malaysia.

▷ In September 1997 children in Kuala Lumpur, Malaysia, wore masks to protect them from breathing in harmful smog.

Profile

Diana, Princess of Wales

After the end of her unhappy marriage to Prince Charles, the Princess of Wales became a popular ambassador worldwide. Among other good causes, she worked for people with AIDS and, in 1996, she travelled to Bosnia and Angola to publicize the campaign against landmines. In August 1997 she died in a car crash. Thousands expressed their grief by leaving flowers and letters outside Kensington Palace, her home in London, and millions watched her funeral. In an extraordinary speech her brother, Earl Spencer, criticized both the press and the royal family for ill-treating her.

△ *Angola, February 1997: Princess Diana talks with landmine victims – a young girl and two former soldiers.*

European Union

In 1992, the 12 countries of the European Community signed the Maastricht Treaty. This moved them closer towards economic and monetary union. The Danish people opposed this in a referendum, but changed their decision in 1993. Conservative ministers in Britain fell out over closer ties with Europe, causing rifts in the government. In 1995, Austria, Finland and Sweden joined the European Community, but Norway decided not to, so there were now 15 members in all.

▽ *French President François Mitterrand (left) and German Chancellor Helmut Kohl led moves towards European integration. In 1993 a 'single market' was created. This enabled goods and workers to move freely between EC countries.*

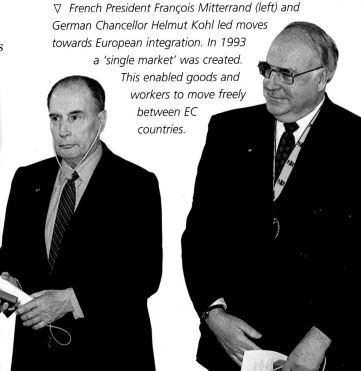

...Newsflash...

Brussels, 1 January 1999. A new currency, the euro, comes into use in 11 European countries today. Britain and Denmark have opted out, while Sweden and Greece were not ready. At first, the euro will be used only for official transactions between banks. Coins and notes will be issued in 2002, replacing national currencies.

A new era

In Britain, on 1 May 1997, a landslide election victory for the Labour Party ended 18 years of Conservative government. Tony Blair became the youngest prime minister for 185 years. He promised to raise standards in schools, and to reform the House of Lords. 119 women MPs joined the House of Commons, by far the highest number ever. After referendums, Scotland gained its own parliament, and Wales an assembly.

In France, Lionel Jospin led the socialists to victory in 1997. A year later, a coalition of Social Democrats and the Green Party came to power in Germany. For the first time ever, the major countries of Europe had broadly left-of-centre governments at the same time, led by a new generation of leaders born since the Second World War.

The Clinton years

In 1992 Bill Clinton defeated George Bush to become president of the USA. The first Democrat president for 12 years, he was especially popular with women and black voters. The economy did well, more people had jobs, and crime was reduced. However, a Republican Party majority

...Newsflash...

Littleton, Denver, 21 April 1999. When two teenagers walked into Columbine High School yesterday, shooting dead a teacher and 12 students before killing themselves, they left this city numb with horror. As after previous massacres, the National Rifle Association states that people, not guns, are to blame. But surely Americans will now rethink their devotion to guns. The makers of violent movies and video games must also be held responsible for the fantasies they fuel in disturbed young minds.

◁ *Tony Blair with South African President Nelson Mandela. After a general election in June 1999, Mandela retired. The new president was Thabo Mbeki.*

in Congress blocked Clinton's attempts to reform health care, introduce gun controls, and curb the powerful tobacco industry. In 1998 the Republicans moved to impeach the president after he lied on oath about his affair with White House worker Monica Lewinsky. The Senate narrowly backed Clinton, and his presidency survived.

▷ *At President Clinton's impeachment trial in February 1999, the Senate considered videotaped recordings of the president being questioned by the Grand Jury.*

A LOOK AT
SCIENCE and TECHNOLOGY
IN THE '90s

In the 1990s, scientific research was aimed at learning more about DNA, the chemical that genes are made of. DNA carries the code that gives each living thing its particular characteristics.

Understanding DNA makes it possible to change or control those characteristics, or even to produce clones (exact copies) of living things from material in their cells. These developments caused moral and practical concern, since they gave humans the means to act upon nature in an entirely new way.

Mapping the genome

The total of all the DNA in a living thing is called its genome. The sequence in which this chemical material is arranged makes a master plan for every life form – animal, plant, or microbe.

4 December 1998. British and US scientists announced today that they have completed identifying the blueprint for a complex, multi-celled organism, the nematode worm. The worm is 1 mm long, but contains more than 97 million bits of DNA and 19,000 genes. The genes are what make the worm squirm, eat and reproduce – they hold the instructions that make the worm what it is. This research has taken 15 years. It brings nearer the day when the blueprint for wheat, or a fish, or a pig may be known.

Profile

Dolly the Sheep

In 1997, researchers at the Roslin Institute, Edinburgh, announced that they had produced the first ever clone of an adult animal. They took a single cell from an adult sheep, and placed its genetic material in an unfertilized ovum (egg cell) which had been stripped of its own DNA. This was then placed inside a female sheep, who became its surrogate (replacement) mother. When the baby sheep was born it was an exact copy of the sheep from which the original cell had been taken. They named her Dolly and she quickly became the world's most photographed animal.

▽ A forensic scientist takes a blood sample from some clothing, to make an 'autorad(iograph)' of the DNA. 'Autorads' are used in a similar way to fingerprints.

The process of working out the DNA sequence is called 'mapping'. First, scientists mapped the DNA of single-cell organisms, including yeast and certain bacteria which cause illness in humans. In December 1998 they revealed that they had mapped a multi-cell organism for the first time. In 1990, scientists from many countries began a project to map the *human* genome.

Using genetic knowledge

The uses of knowledge about genetics became clear as the decade progressed. The police identified criminals from DNA in a single hair or traces of blood or saliva. The precise genes associated with certain inherited illnesses were identified; this led to the development of more reliable medical tests and treatment. But such advances had drawbacks too. Would it spoil a person's life to know that he or she carried a hidden disease – especially if there was no cure? Would insurance companies expect people to have genetic tests before taking out health or life insurance?

Genetically modified crops

Farmers in the USA, China, Argentina and Canada began to grow genetically modified soya, cotton and maize, on a large scale. They used seed produced

▷ These melons have been genetically modified to give off less gas than they do naturally (the tubes are checking this). The melons now ripen more slowly and so last longer.

In his book 'The Genetic Revolution', Dr Patrick Dixon urged all people to become informed:

'If we do not take control of advancing gene technology now, then it will take control of us by changing the very roots of our society and our being.'

and patented by chemical companies. Other countries held back. They were concerned that GM foods could harm human or animal health, and that pollen from GM crops might contaminate other crops or wildlife. They asked whose interest this new science served.

▷ *Greenpeace activists in France cut down GM maize, in a protest action, September 1998.*

Some GM seeds were 'suicide seeds': they were made with a terminator gene inside so that the next generation of seeds would be sterile. This meant that farmers would have to buy new seed each year rather than saving their own. Before long, could the world's major crops all be under the control of a handful of private firms? As the decade ended, farmers in India and Brazil campaigned against being forced to use GM seeds. In Britain, supermarkets ceased stocking foods containing GM ingredients.

Food scares

People were suspicious about new methods of food production for other reasons too. Scientists had disagreed about whether BSE, a terrible disease that broke out in British cattle, could be passed to humans through eating beef. In 1996 they admitted it could, and that some people had died as a result. Hundreds of thousands of cows had to be destroyed.

In the USA and 16 other countries, cows were regularly injected with BST, a man-made hormone, to increase the amount of milk they produced. In Europe use of the hormone was banned. It was said to damage the animals' health and pose a threat to human health, too.

Computers and the Internet

All through the 1990s computers brought change to the ways in which people lived and worked. Businesses and public services relied more and more on computers, linked through complex networks, to handle vast amounts of information. Instead of working in small local offices or banks, more people worked in large call centres dealing with telephone calls from customers far and wide. Computers

◁ *Billionaire chairman of Microsoft, Bill Gates (left) stands by as TV presenter Jay Leno helps him launch his new Microsoft system, Windows 95, in August 1995.*

underpinned international trade, speeding up the way money and stocks and shares were moved around. Since so many workers were expected to be computer-literate, schools increasingly taught information technology. At home, people used personal computers, the Internet and e-mail.

As computing developed, certain companies became famous for particular applications. IBM had led the way with spreadsheets, and Macintosh with desk-top publishing. In the 1990s the dominant company was Microsoft. Its distinctive product was a versatile software system called 'Windows', which could be used with all IBM-compatible computers. In 1998, other companies challenged Microsoft in the US courts, for blocking fair competition.

◁ Buzz Lightyear (left) and Woody were two characters in 'Toy Story', the first feature-length film to be created entirely by computer animation, 1995.

The 'Millennium Bug'

Another problem was far more troublesome. It arose because of the coming change of dates in the year 2000. Many computers used only the last two digits of a four-digit year date. They would be likely to misinterpret a date which would register only as '00', and this could cause whole systems to crash. The potential problem and the chaos that might follow had been recognized for years. But efforts to put matters right only gathered pace as the year 2000 approached. They involved reprogramming computer systems around the world, and cost billions of pounds.

Bugs and viruses

In 1992, computer users first became aware of the danger of computer viruses. These could enter a computer's central system through contact with material from another computer. The bug then cancelled out, or made nonsense of information stored on the computer's hard disk. In March 1992 the 'Michelangelo' virus did exactly this to many computers across the world. It had been designed to do so by a prankster. Experts had to watch for new viruses and created software to get rid of them.

Films and TV

Developments in the way computers could transform images meant that photographs and film could be manipulated in new and convincing ways. These techniques were used to enhance the original special effects in the *Star Wars* films, reissued in 1997, and to make the film *Babe*.

By the end of the 1990s digital television created the potential for a better-quality TV picture and sound. It meant more channels, though not necessarily better programmes.

...Newsflash...

Black Rock, Nevada, 25 September 1997. The world land speed record was broken here earlier today. RAF pilot Andy Green, driving his *Thrust* ssc jet car, completed two two-mile-long runs at an average of 714 mph. This was 81 mph faster than the previous record. Then *Thrust* broke the sound barrier at 763 mph, a feat many people thought could never be achieved on land.

▷ *Comet Hale Bopp, with its two tails, glides over Varna, Bulgaria, 12 March 1997. The comet was clearly visible through much of the northern hemisphere, at dawn and dusk during March 1997. Named after two astronomers, it was four times larger than the famous Halley's Comet.*

▽ *Gas pillars in the Eagle Nebula – an image sent to earth by the Hubble Space Telescope in November 1995.*

Exploration of space

The USA and Russia still led the exploration of space, but now it was on a more cooperative basis. Astronauts from both countries, and from Britain, worked on the space station MIR. In June 1997 there was concern when a supply ship collided with the elderly MIR, damaging the solar panels that provided power. Three astronauts were stranded in darkness with little oxygen. But they managed to make repairs. In 1998 the first module of a new international space station – the US-financed, Russian-built Zarya – was launched.

Extraordinarily detailed images of events in space were provided by the Hubble Space Telescope, launched in 1990 to study the origin of the universe. There was also excitement when NASA's Pathfinder probe landed on Mars on 4 July 1997. It transmitted pictures of the planet's surface, but there was still no proof that life had ever existed there.

Transport and technology

Because of concern about the pollution caused by car fumes, low-pollution cars using petrol and batteries combined were being developed. Some people believed that fuel-cell electric cars were just a few years away. These would use hydrogen from methanol to produce an electric current. Some new vehicles contained a tracking system that informed the driver of road conditions ahead. But governments increasingly acknowledged the need to develop high-quality public transport as an alternative to cars. France led the way with its fabulous high-speed trains. In Denmark, Europe's longest rail and motor-way bridge (6.6 km) was opened in 1994. The 5-km Severn Crossing, a new bridge opened in 1996 between England and Wales, became the longest in Britain.

Mountain bikes became popular in the early 1990s, mountains or not! But in the 1992 Olympics a revolutionary, high-tec racing bike stole the show. Built with a carbon-fibre frame to an unusual design, it helped Chris Boardman win gold in the 4,000 metres. In 1998, the Green Tyre Company, based in Britain, was invited to Shanghai, China, to help supply the half a billion cycles used there. Its polyurethane tyres contain foam instead of air. When worn out, they can be ground up and used to make new tyres.

▽ *With so many people on the move, mobile phones were used widely. However, evidence gathered that constant use could cause headaches, and even serious brain disease.*

...Newsflash...

6 May 1994. Trains are now running through the Channel Tunnel! Having opened a passenger terminal at London's Waterloo Station, Queen Elizabeth II travelled through the Tunnel to join President Mitterrand for a ribbon-cutting ceremony in France. The tunnel is a huge feat of engineering and technology. It was in October 1990 that the drillers from both countries first broke through with a 5-cm pilot hole. Two months later they met face to face. The high-speed train journey on Eurostar from London to Paris takes just three hours. Cars and lorries do not drive through but are transported on le Shuttle.

A LOOK AT
FASHION
IN THE '90s

No single look dominated the decade, but the trend was towards softer, slender styles. Most clothes were understated, and the exaggerated shoulder pads and power dressing of the 1980s were definitely out. Women's clothes were less structured, and the fabrics more tactile.

In the mid-1990s some dresses were even deliberately made to look like lingerie, and the trouser suit for women returned. In 1998, skirts for men appeared – though only a few were brave enough to wear them.

Making a statement
Young women wore tight, figure-revealing tops, with 1960s-style mini-skirts; or with floating Hippie-style skirts or trousers, cut low to sit below the waist rather than on it. With these clothes often went long, loose hair styles. Many also wore tough-looking foot-wear, seeming to state that girls could be anything they chose to be.

△ *Fleece jackets and miniature rucksacks turned the outward-bound look into city fashion.*

New fabrics
Softer, body-revealing styles were achieved partly by the use of new stretchy, shiny fabrics containing Lycra.

Just about everyone bought a fleece – a soft, unlined jacket made from synthetic fabric, which combined snug warmth with almost no weight. Developed

◁ *Dr Martens boots (originally made as strong black leather working boots with reinforced toes) became a fashion item for young men and women. These dancers were part of the publicity for the opening of a shop in London selling nothing but 'Docs', in every imaginable colour.*

Profile

John Galliano

Son of a south London plumber, John Galliano led the way for a new generation of British clothes designers who came to dominate the world of fashion in the 1990s. He studied at Central St Martin's College, London, and was soon designing clothes full of flair and imagination. In 1996 he showed his first haute couture collection for the Paris fashion house Givenchy. After that he went to be head designer at Christian Dior.

◁ *John Galliano on the catwalk with a model at his 1997-98 ready-to-wear fashion show in Paris.*

originally for sports wear and outdoor pursuits, fleece had the great advantage of being machine-washable. As part of this casual, comfortable style, most people owned a pair of trainers, and the fashion status that trainers achieved in the late 1980s lingered on.

Towards the end of the '90s there was a revival of clothes decorated with beading.

'Cool Britannia'

No one is sure who said it first, but suddenly Britain became 'cool Britannia'. US magazines ran features explaining that London was the place to be – the new fashion capital of the world. Praise was heaped on young British designers John Galliano, Alexander McQueen and Stella McCartney. They had all graduated from London's Central St Martin's College of Art and Design. Each of them was appointed to design collections for French fashion houses, though they maintained their own labels too. They took the world of fashion by storm with their extravagant fashion shows and eye-catching clothes.

◁ *One of Alexander McQueen's concepts for the London Fashion Show, 1997.*

Spectacular shows

Fashion shows introduce new designs to wealthy customers and buyers from major stores. Most of all they are aimed at the world's press. In the 1990s, shows were staged as dramatic events. Unusual locations and themes were chosen to shock, or to grab the headlines. By the end of the 1990s critics were saying that the shows were all spectacle and no substance, and that the clothes were impossible to wear. But as always, designer fashion did influence the clothes that later appeared in the shops.

Reporting on London Fashion Week in 1998, Tamsin Blanchard wrote that many clothes were

'made by self-indulgent designers who should know by now that no woman wants to look like a) a sci-fi hero, b) a drag queen, c) a freak.'

▷ Super-models like Claudia Schiffer were paid huge sums in return for adding their names and images to all kinds of products.

Models and advertising

Top fashion models such as Linda Evangelista, Cindy Crawford, Naomi Campbell, Kate Moss and Claudia Schiffer, became rich and famous. But some people criticized magazines and agencies for the fact that models

Profile

Naomi Campbell

'Supermodels' were a small group of models who became international stars, famous way beyond the world of fashion. Britain's Naomi Campbell was the only black woman among them. She had a winning personality and extremely long legs, and looked as good in glamorous catwalk oufits as in street-style clothes. Naomi was 19 when she appeared on the front cover of *Vogue* magazine in 1990. She rapidly became very famous. High session fees and advertising contracts made her extremely wealthy. A book about her life is titled *The Rise and Rise of the Girl from Nowhere*.

were always unusually tall, super-thin, and in some cases quite ill-looking. Comparing themselves with these models made people unhappy with their own shape, and could lead to harmful dieting and eating disorders.

Posters advertising Benetton clothes showed images unrelated to fashion. They were chosen to shock – for example, a man dying from AIDS. Many people said such advertising was exploitative and distasteful.

Variations of black

In spite of the hype, most people stuck to unflashy clothes and colours for everyday wear. Black was worn for office work and evening wear, until people tired of it. In 1997 brown was declared the 'new black' – only to be replaced in 1998 by grey, also called the new black! That year Italian designer Armani produced restrained and elegant trouser suits and dresses, all in grey.

...Newsflash...

Paris, 16 October 1998. Japanese designer Issey Miyake surprised the fashion world with his new collection this week. His show opened with three men cutting garments out of a tube of cloth laid on the catwalk. Every garment in the show had been produced the same way. A-POC (a piece of cloth) will hit the shops next summer – tubes of cloth in rainbow colours, marked with dotted lines. Miyake customers will then cut out their own clothes to suit their size, shape and preference.

◁ *Some people chose to have a stud or ring in their navel.*

Body-piercing and tattoos

Body-piercing and tattoos were popular among young people, especially girls. Studs decorated ears, eyebrows, noses and navels. Some people even went as far as getting their tongues pierced. The fashion caused concern, because when carried out inexpertly it could lead to infection or disfigurement.

▷ *Tennis star André Agassi made his own fashion statement on court. His shorts were baggy, in the style of trousers popular among young black men in the USA. His shirts were cut short at the front to show a flash of tummy when he served.*

A LOOK AT
MUSIC
IN THE '90s

At the start of the 1990s, a revival of 1960s sounds was underway. A flourishing music scene existed in Seattle, USA. In the 1960s, this city had produced Janis Joplin and Jimi Hendrix. Now from Seattle came rock band Nirvana, their music associated with hard living and drug taking. The sad fate which ended the lives of the earlier stars seemed to catch up with Nirvana's lead singer Kurt Cobain, who committed suicide in 1994.

In Britain the city to watch was Manchester. Liam and Noel Gallagher grew up there. They unashamedly based their band, Oasis, on the Beatles, who had also been northern and working-class. Oasis performed their own material. They were rebels, and spoke for a new generation. Their main rivals were Blur, a band from London.

For a time in Britain music formed part of a protest against the Criminal Justice Act, which was introduced to prevent large 'rave' parties. In October 1994, 100,000 young protesters gathered in London's Hyde Park to defy the Act.

▽ *Noel and Liam Gallagher of Oasis, at a concert in 1996.*

Profile

Michael Jackson

Michael Jackson (seen here in 1997) was a supreme showman, singer and dancer. In 1991 he launched his single and video *Black or White* and began a world tour. His skin was white and his features had changed. In a rare TV interview with Oprah Winfrey, he said his pale skin was caused by a disease. But his personal behaviour remained secretive and strange. He issued *History*, a double album and video costing $50 million to make, in 1995. In 1996 he made a video in the slums of Rio de Janeiro, *They Don't Really Care About Us*.

Profile

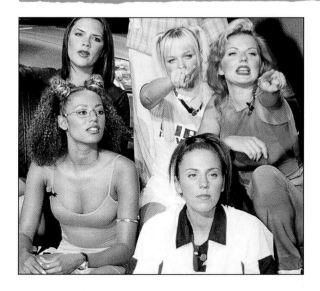

The Spice Girls

British girl band the Spice Girls topped the singles charts in 28 countries in 1996, and never looked back. Their energetic songs and dance routines became hugely famous. Individually they were known as Scary, Sporty, Posh, Baby and Ginger Spice. Ginger Spice (Geri Halliwell) left the group in 1998, and completely changed her image. She was appointed to work for the United Nations as a goodwill ambassador. The other Spice Girls carried on, even after two announced that they were having babies.

Rap artists, such as Puff Daddy, produced successful songs with a distinctive style. But some rap was criticized for its violent and sexist lyrics. Dance music flourished in late-night clubs, which led revivals of disco, hip-hop and indie music. Club culture became associated with the use of a drug called ecstasy. A number of young people died from using it.

Boy and girl bands
The biggest worldwide stars were the Spice Girls, with their 'girl power'. Bands such as Take That, the Back Street Boys and All Saints were also popular with teenage fans. Take That's Robbie Williams went on to be a major solo star.

▷ *Puff Daddy (left) in Los Angeles, 1998.*

66 99

At the 1996 Brit Awards, Jarvis Cocker, lead singer of Pulp, tried to interrupt Michael Jackson's performance of 'Earth Song'. He explained:

'My actions were a form of protest at the way Michael Jackson sees himself as some Christ-like figure with the power of healing. The music industry allows him to indulge his fantasies.'

European success

Some distinctive new stars emerged in the smaller countries of Europe. Ireland was experiencing new prosperity and cultural change. Its music scene, including U2 and the Cranberries, reflected this. Most famous individual performer was the gifted Sinead O'Connor, with her emotional songs and shaved head. But she was booed from the stage in New York, after her outspoken criticism of the Catholic Church. Ireland also produced the Corrs, boy band Boyzone, and girl band B*witched. From Sweden came Ace of Base.

The annual Eurovision Song Contest was watched by a TV audience of millions. Many enjoyed the contest for the amusement given by some songs being so bad, and the voting of the national juries being so biased! In the 1990s, Irish musicians ran away with the prize so frequently that success became a financial embarrassment: the winning country must always host the event the following year.

△ *Talented and original female singer, Bjork, seen here in 1996, is from Iceland.*

In tune with the times

A performance at the football World Cup tournament, in Italy, 1990, featuring 'Nessun Dorma!' from Puccini's opera *Turandot*, led to worldwide popularity for famous opera singers Placido Domingo, Jose Carreras and Luciano Pavarotti. As 'The Three Tenors', they issued albums, and sang again at the World Cup tournaments in the USA, 1994, and France,1998. Together they created a new audience for operatic arias.

The Euro '96 tournament in England inspired another musical success. TV comics David Baddiel and Frank Skinner wrote a song with the chorus 'Football's coming home'. Titled 'Three Lions', and recorded by The Lightning Seeds, it became a classic popular anthem. In a decade when football players rivalled pop stars as popular heroes, Posh Spice and her boyfriend England player David Beckham were a fashionable couple.

◁ *The 1998 Danish grammy winners Aqua had a huge hit with their ironic song 'Barbie Girl'.*

...Newsflash...

14 September 1997. Elton John's recording of 'Candle in the Wind', released yesterday, sold 600,000 copies in that one day! This makes it the fastest-selling single ever. Elton John rewrote the song, which he had originally penned in memory of Marilyn Monroe, as a memorial to Diana, Princess of Wales, who had been a personal friend. He performed the song at her funeral in Westminster Abbey, accompanying himself on the piano. All the money raised by sales of the record are to go to the Diana Memorial Fund.

△ *Young violinists Nigel Kennedy and Vanessa Mae (above) did not conform to the usual ways of classical musicians. Their flamboyant looks and style gave a new image to the music they performed.*

Old-timers

In the 1960s, rock music had been performed by and for young people. Whilst the people had grown older, there was proof now that the music of their younger days could last. The 1990s began with a huge success for established Canadian singer Bryan Adams, with '(Everything I Do) I Do it for You'. Some of the '90s young generation found that they liked the Beatles and Bob Dylan. Sixties albums were re-released on CD, with the recordings cleaned up and sounding remarkably fresh. Bruce Springsteen, Van Morrison, The Rolling Stones and Cliff Richard were still performing live to big audiences. In 1998, 52-year-old singer Cher went straight to the top of the charts with her new single, 'Believe'.

◁ *Glastonbury, 1998. Outdoor rock festivals grew larger and more commercial in the 1990s. Young people camped out, sometimes in appalling weather, to enjoy the music.*

A LOOK AT
ART and ARCHITECTURE
IN THE '90s

Painting seemed to take a 'back seat' to other forms of visual art, such as sculpture, in the 1990s. The decade may be remembered for large-scale, outdoor projects.

In 1993, sixteen giant sculptures by Fernando Botero graced Park Avenue, New York. In 1998, extraordinary, gigantic figures were created and paraded through the streets of Paris for the opening of the World Cup. In Britain, Antony Gormley's sculpture the 'Angel of the North', with enormous outstretched wings, was erected outside Newcastle. It was a mixture of aeronautics and anatomy.

" "

Sculptor Antony Gormley said:

'any piece of work in the late twentieth century has to speak to the whole world.'

▷ *Ho, Pablo, Moussa and Romeo, the figures paraded through Paris for the opening of the World Cup, represented the continents. Ho (right) symbolized Asia.*

Most of Gormley's sculptures were based on the human form. He used the technique of plastering over live models, including himself, to explore the space inside a person, as well as the outer form. In 1992 he exhibited 'Field', an assembly of some 35,000 terracotta figures that filled art galleries and spilled through the doorways. As well as appearing to have a unique personality, each figure also expressed the imprint of a person's hands, as it was moulded between palms and fingers. None was more then two hands high.

Photography

News photography was transformed by technical advances that enabled newspapers to print colour photographs to a high standard. But photojournalist Sebastiao Salgado preferred the drama and contrast of photographs in black and white. His striking portraits and action shots of poor and downtrodden people in many countries gave his subjects dignity and power. In particular, he recorded the struggle of miners and landless peasants in Brazil, the country where he was born. Salgado's epic images were exhibited and acclaimed around the world.

A retrospective exhibition enhanced the reputation of Eve Arnold, veteran US photographer of both the famous and the obscure. In contrast, the work of Annie Leibovitz came under scrutiny. Her glossy celebrity portraits had graced the covers of the fashion magazine *Vanity Fair* in the 1980s, making her the USA's highest-paid photographer. They were colourful and stylized, but some critics thought them slick and false. In the 1990s she worked on some less commercial projects, including photographing Sarajevo during the conflict in former Yugoslavia.

Painting

Although many young artists were not working with paint, one artist in particular used paint with exuberance. Howard Hodgkin's

△ Inside the dome of the new parliament (Reichstag) building in Berlin – designed by architect Norman Foster and opened in 1999.

modernist paintings brimmed with bright colour and brushstrokes. Often the paint burst right over the picture frames. In the art market, high prices were paid for paintings by Francis Bacon, who died in 1992, and by Lucian Freud.

One of the most influential collectors of art was Charles Saatchi, a wealthy advertising executive. His buying power made him an important patron of young British artists such as Damien Hirst and Rachel Whiteread. Damien Hirst achieved notoriety with his 'installations', sometimes featuring dead animals preserved in formaldehyde. In 1997, an important art show titled 'Sensation' brought this work to an international audience.

◁ Damien Hirst with one of his installations entitled 'Mother and Child', at the Tate Gallery, London, 1995.

Architecture

Some self-confident, highly original public buildings were built in the 1990s, including major museums and galleries. This was a change from the 1980s, when commercial buildings such as banks and shopping malls predominated. Architects experimented with how a building encloses space, and with the use of natural light. They used new materials and giddy, unexpected shapes.

Spain leads the way

Spain's economic and democratic progress was displayed when it hosted Expo '92 in Seville. With 102 nations participating, 58 national and 5 shared pavilions were erected. A new city with bold architecture and gardens was developed on the island of Cartuja, plus a new airport and high-speed rail link with Madrid. Architect Ricardo Bofill designed the airport and the National Theatre of Catalunya.

The world's highest building, the Petronas Towers in Kuala Lumpur, Malaysia, was completed shortly before the Asian economic crisis of August 1997. In the USA,

▽ *In the Basque city of Bilbao, northern Spain, the futuristic Guggenheim Museum took shape. Covered in glittering titanium, it was immediately hailed as the masterpiece building of the twentieth century. The architect, Frank Gehry, also designed the Weisman Museum in Minneapolis.*

...Newsflash...

London, 25 June 1998. After years of construction work, the new British Library designed by Colin St John Wilson has been formally opened by the Queen. Britain's largest public building this century, it cost £511 million. As well as books, maps and manuscripts held on open shelves on three floors above ground, 12 million volumes will be stored on 300 kilometres of shelves in four levels of underground basements. There are advanced systems for protection from fire and flood. A network of conveyors and lifts delivers books to readers throughout the building.

Profile

Norman Foster

Norman Foster's work won worldwide acclaim. His earlier buildings, including Stansted Airport and the Sainsbury Gallery at the University of East Anglia, seemed to celebrate natural light and space. In the 1990s he designed the new parliament building in Berlin, and was chosen to design the new assembly for Wales. His American Air Museum at Duxford, Cambridge-shire, won an award in 1998. It was judged 'a great big, clear-span building beautifully integrated into its flat landscape, cunningly daylit around its perimeter, and with a virtuoso roof ... from which the planes are suspended'.

▷ *The Petronas Towers in Kuala Lumpur stand in a park designed to be a haven for tropical flora and fauna.*

new buildings at Arizona State University were praised, as were the Seattle Art Museum and the Tennessee Aquarium, Chatanooga. In Australia, Gregory Burgess designed unusual unobtrusive buildings to be used as aboriginal cultural centres.

As the 1990s ended, Berlin was being transformed into a new capital city for Germany, perhaps a cultural centre for all Europe. As well as the new parliament building (page 27), a new railway station was taking shape – Europe's biggest – boasting a 430-metre glass concourse, 58 escalators and 37 lifts. Meanwhile, in Britain, the coming of the 21st century was celebrated by the building of a Millennium Dome, designed by Richard Rogers, to look like a giant spacecraft which had landed close to the meridian at Greenwich.

A LOOK AT

SPORT

IN THE '90s

Sport was more prominent in people's lives than ever. Millions watched, and, with a growing number of television channels, some dedicated entirely to sport, even minor sports found an audience. For others, sport was a matter of business. Football and tennis, and in the USA baseball and basketball, became highly profitable industries. Famous clubs were quoted on the stock exchange. Sports management courses were popular in colleges, and careers opened up. Finally there were those who took part, as either professionals or amateurs.

▷ *At the Olympic Games in Atlanta, 1996, Kerri Strug was part of the US Women's Gymnastics Team, which won gold.*

Marathons

Men and women participated at all levels of ability in marathons held in cities around the world. Some were sponsored for charity. Some took part as disabled competitors. Among the winners, black African runners dominated, in the tradition of their Olympic successes in earlier decades. In the London marathon held in 1997, 29,000 competitors took part, a record for any race anywhere.

Goodbye

Gary Lineker (England); Franco Baresi (Italy); Diego Maradona (Argentina); Jurgen Klinsman (Germany)

Hello

Ronaldo (Brazil); Zinedine Zidane (France); George Weah (Liberia); Alessandro del Piero (Italy); Michael Owen (England); Peter Schmeichel (Denmark)

Football – worldwide

Thanks to satellite TV, famous clubs such as Manchester United or Barcelona had fans as far away as Africa and China. As audiences grew, football changed from being a sport mainly of interest to working-class men. Grounds and facilities were improved, and the game became fashionable. During three World Cup tournaments in 1990, 1994 and 1998, it seemed that whole populations were caught up in following their national teams. Football, or soccer, even grew in the USA, which hosted the

...Newsflash...

Gothenburg, 26 June 1992.
In a fairytale story worthy of Hans Christian Andersen, Denmark's under-rated football team have beaten World Cup holders Germany 2 – 0 to win the European Championship. Denmark was only invited to play in the tournament ten days before its start, when Yugoslavia was banned from taking part for violation of human rights. On their way to the final the Danes also overcame the teams from France and Holland.

▷
In the 1994 World Cup final, Italy's Roberto Baggio hangs his head after missing a penalty kick. This miss, in front of a 94,000 crowd in Pasadena, meant that Italy lost to Brazil. It was the first time that a World Cup final had been decided on penalties.

1994 World Cup. Interest was especially high in communities in the USA that originated from Italy or South America.

Top players and managers could command high salaries all round the world. Big clubs made fortunes from sponsorship and television broadcast rights. Also highly profitable was the sale of home and away strips, which the clubs changed regularly to keep fans buying!

Profile

Eric Cantona

French footballer Cantona played in the English premier league, winning hearts with his football skills and passionate temperament. He received a temporary ban in 1995, after aiming a kung fu-style kick at a spectator who shouted racist remarks. But he returned to captain Manchester United to the league and cup double. Cantona once said: 'Football is the most beautiful of the arts.' He published a book of his thoughts and sayings. Cantona led his team to another premiership title in 1997. Afterwards he retired and became a film actor.

◁ Jonah Lomu storms forward in the All Blacks' match against England, 1997. 1.95m tall, weighing 118 kg, and with size 14.5 boots, he was hard to stop!

South Africa returns to world sport

Some of the political problems that bedevilled sport in earlier decades had faded. For years South African sport had been boycotted by other countries, because it was run on racial lines. The change of government in South Africa meant that sports previously reserved for whites also had to accept change. Now South African teams were welcomed back into world sport.

In June 1995, South Africa hosted and won the Rugby World Cup. The South African team beat the New Zealand All Blacks – including star player Jonah Lomu – in a thrilling final. President Mandela joined the celebrations, as the colourful new South African flag was waved. It marked a unifying moment in a country where sport is almost a religion.

...Newsflash...

Southern Ocean, 7 January 1997. Lone yachtsman Tony Bullimore, aged 57, was rescued today after surviving five days trapped in his upturned yacht in the world's most remote waters. He was taking part in a round-the-world solo yacht race when his craft, *Exide Challenger*, capsized in heavy seas, 2,200 km south of Australia. He lay trapped in darkness in the cabin, in a pocket of air above the freezing water. The air had almost run out when he was rescued by an Australian frigate.

Profile

Michael Jordan

Raised in North Carolina, 1.98 metres tall, with a fantastic ability to leap through the air, Michael Jordan became the pre-eminent basketball player of the 1990s. He was a member of the US team that won Olympic gold in 1992. Playing for the Chicago Bulls, he averaged 41 points a game in their record-breaking run of three championships, 1991-93. The sportswear company Nike paid huge sums to name a type of trainer 'Nike Air Jordans' after him. Jordan retired from basketball in 1999.

Golden days in Atlanta

The 1996 Olympics, in Atlanta, USA, were the largest games ever. 11,000 athletes from 197 nations took part, and events were screened live to audiences around the world, who witnessed some record-breaking performances.

Kerri Strug competed with a damaged ankle to help the US gymnastics team win gold, and runner Michael Johnson won the 400 metres and 200 metres, breaking a world record that had stood for 17 years. Nigeria became the first ever African team to win gold in the football competition, while Josia Thugware, who won the men's marathon, was the first black South African to win Olympic gold.

Perhaps most remarkable of all was the achievement of 34-year-old Steve Redgrave, the British oarsman, who with his partner Matthew Pinsent won gold in the coxless pairs. It was Redgrave's fourth successive Olympic gold and afterwards he joked: 'I've had enough. If anyone sees me go near a boat they have my permission to shoot me.' But a few months later he began to train for the Sydney 2000 Olympics. No one in Olympic history has won gold at five successive Olympic Games – yet.

Sports commentators asked:

'Have the Olympic Games become too big and too commercial? And now that sports like synchronized swimming and beach volley-ball have been included, where will it all end?'

◁ *The 1994 Winter Olympics were held in Norway and brought 2 million visitors to the country – equal to half the country's population. Norway topped the medals table, and Norwegian speed skater Johann Koss set three new world records.*

◁ Cyclists in the 1998 Tour de France staged a strike in protest at the way the French police had taken some participants to hospital for drug tests. Danish cyclist Bjarne Riis acted as spokesman.

Athletes challenged the accuracy of drug tests through the courts. One lawyer said:

'There is evidence that an adverse finding can be caused by nandrolone naturally occurring in the body, by supplements not on the banned list or by meat products.'

Problems with drugs

Unfortunately, some athletes resorted to taking drugs to boost their performance, and so brought their sports into disrepute. Drug scandals nearly wrecked the famous Tour de France cycle race in 1998.

The effects of sudden fame and fast lifestyles also caused problems. Use of so-called recreational drugs interrupted the careers of tennis player Jennifer Capriati and footballer Diego Maradona. British player Tony Adams went to prison for driving when drunk. He had the courage to admit that he was an alcoholic, received help to stop drinking, and went on to captain Arsenal and England. He later supported Paul Gascoigne and other players whose careers were threatened by alcohol addiction.

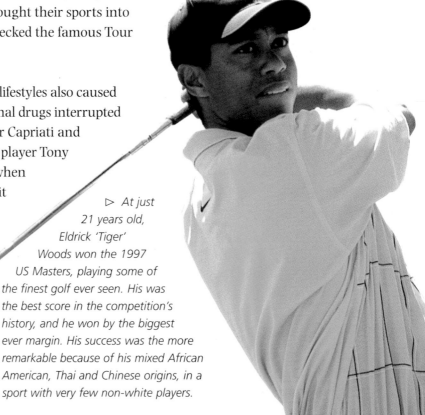

▷ At just 21 years old, Eldrick 'Tiger' Woods won the 1997 US Masters, playing some of the finest golf ever seen. His was the best score in the competition's history, and he won by the biggest ever margin. His success was the more remarkable because of his mixed African American, Thai and Chinese origins, in a sport with very few non-white players.

Tennis

Supreme champion of the 1990s was Pete Sampras of the USA, with his serve and volley game. André Agassi and Goran Ivanisevic rose through the ranks, while Boris Becker was still a force to be reckoned with. Britain, for so long without top-class players, now had Greg Rusedski and Tim Henman in the world's top ten. There was concern that the game had been spoiled by new-style racquets. These made shots harder and faster, but reduced delicate 'touch' play and the number and length of rallies. In response, tennis authorities altered the weight of the ball, to slow it down.

Martina Navratilova retired in 1994 with a career total of 167 singles titles. She had dominated the game for so long that three years later Martina Hingis, who had been named after Navratilova, won her first Wimbledon title! Up to then, Steffi Graf and Monica Seles led women's tennis.

△ In 1997, 16-year-old Martina Hingis from Switzerland became the youngest Wimbledon champion of the century. She also won the US Open and Australian titles.

...Newsflash...

Edgbaston, 6 June 1994. What a great year this is for cricket! In February, Kapil Dev took his 432nd test wicket in India's test against Sri Lanka. In April, left-handed West Indies batsman Brian Lara hooked England's Chris Lewis for a boundary, to pass Sir Garfield Sobers' record test score of 365 not out. Lara finally fell at 375. Today, playing for Warwickshire against Durham, Lara ended his innings 501 not out, the highest ever total in first-class cricket. Will English schools be inspired to revive cricket? They must, if England is ever to match the strength of India, Pakistan, Australia and the West Indies.

In a horrific incident in 1993, a crazed spectator stabbed Seles on court in Hamburg. She recovered and began a successful comeback two years later.

Baseball

In August 1994, baseball players in the USA went on strike for more pay. Team owners responded by calling off the whole season. In 1998, Roger Maris's 37-year-old home run record was broken by Sammy Sosa. He scored 66 for the Chicago Cubs. Mark McGwire of the St Louis Cardinals then beat that with 70 home runs in one season.

A LOOK AT
LEISURE and ENTERTAINMENT
IN THE '90s

In the 1990s more and more of the films and television people watched, the books and magazines they read, and even the food they ate, were produced by huge multi-national corporations.

One example was News International, owned by Rupert Murdoch. It controlled TV and film companies, newspapers, publishing houses and sports teams around the world. There was concern that such monopolies threatened cultural diversity, and freedom of expression.

American influence

Now that the Cold War was over, US culture and products were more powerful than ever. The red Coca-Cola logo was said to be the world's most widely recognized symbol. Coca-Cola's arch-rival, Pepsi, spent $500 million on remarketing Pepsi in blue packaging. Themed restaurants such as Planet Hollywood, and the Fashion Café, used their links with celebrities to attract customers, but by the end of the decade their success was fading. Fast-food corporation

△ An inflated figure of Ronald McDonald outside a new McDonalds in Peking, 1994.

Profile

The Simpsons

The Simpsons, an inventive and very funny television cartoon series of the 1990s, took an ironic look at life in the USA. Homer Simpson worked at a nuclear plant. He was a glutton, and a lazy although loving father. Marge, his wife, waged a long-suffering battle to improve her family's manners. Bart, with his rude ways and constant search for street credibility, was completely unlike his sisters, the high-achieving, wise and intellectual Lisa, and baby Maggie. *The Simpsons* was hugely popular with children and adults.

McDonalds grew at an astonishing rate, even opening outlets in Moscow and Peking. The menu, no matter where, was based on sameness and limited choice. It was targeted at young people.

Some people resented the rise of fast-food culture, especially in France with its tradition of fine cooking. But even in France hamburger outlets grew in number. In Europe and the USA, many more mothers went out to work than before. Fewer people cooked at home from raw ingredients. The majority of homes acquired microwaves. Supermarkets sold more and more ready-made meals. At the same time, some people developed a 'foodie' culture, drawing on the best of world cuisine. In London, not previously known for fine food, fashionable restaurants opened. Top chefs became famous. Other celebrity chefs had their own TV series, and their books were best-sellers.

...Newsflash...

London, 19 June 1997. The longest civil trial ever held in Britain has ended after two years. Dave Morris and Helen Street, two environmental activists, have been found guilty of libelling McDonalds in a leaflet which criticized the corporation's products and methods. Morris and Street faced the might of McDonalds and its lawyers without legal assistance, calling witnesses from around the world to support their views. Many people think that the campaigners have won a moral victory by standing up for their opinions. The trial cost McDonalds millions of dollars.

▷ *Line dancing, 1998.*

Dancing
A new craze, American line dancing, caught on among people of all ages. It spread outwards from the USA.

Some line dancers dressed up in Western-style clothes and boots; the moves involved cowboy-style heel-clicking and jumping. It was all great fun, and since everyone danced in a line, you didn't even need a partner!

Meanwhile a spectacular new show called *Riverdance* made Irish dancing popular. Performed to traditional music, Irish dancing involves fast footwork, while the top half of the body stays upright and still.

△ In 'Riverdance', a troupe of men and women danced with military precision, filling the stage with sound and colour.

Theme parks

During the 1990s theme parks, where families could have days out enjoying spectacular rides and exhibits, grew in size and number. In Britain, Alton Towers was the biggest. Lego, makers of the popular toy, opened a Legoland in England, to match the one in Denmark. EuroDisney, later re-launched as Disneyland Paris, opened in France in 1992.

Engineers competed to build the world's biggest, most thrilling rides. They studied aspects of safety, and what forces the average human body can take without coming to harm. 'The Big One', the world's tallest roller-coaster, began operating in Blackpool in 1994, attracting record crowds.

Many British families, used to spending their holidays in Spain, could now afford for the first time to go to the USA. The most

◁ April 1992: a parade during the opening of 'EuroDisney' in Paris.

popular destination was Florida, where Disney World and Universal Studios were booming.

Shopping

Out-of-town shopping malls, common in the USA, had spread to Britain and Europe. In response, some local councils invested in revitalizing town centres, so that they would not become run-down and empty.

In August 1994, Britain finally abandoned its law against Sunday shopping, which many shops had already broken. Supermarkets now stayed open for longer hours – in some cases round-the-clock. Shop assistants worked shifts, and part-time jobs were created. Similarly, some banks provided 24-hour telephone banking, which meant that call-centre workers were on duty all night. Many people welcomed the chance to go shopping any time in the week. But for others, the tradition of families spending Sundays and evenings relaxing together was lost.

In the USA, TV shopping had begun. After seeing goods described, people telephoned their orders using credit cards. Shopping via the Internet was hailed as the thing of the future. It should be possible to order goods on-line, and have them delivered to your door. However, the idea was slow to start. Banks had first to develop security systems, to prevent credit card details being stolen or mis-used.

Computer games

Games could be played on home computers or via television sets with a console. The graphics became very sophisticated. Portable computer games such as Game Boy were popular too. In 1997, there was a craze for Tamagotchi 'virtual pets'. These were small computerized toys from Japan that had to be 'fed' at regular intervals or else they would 'die'. As more homes went on-line, some people spent many hours a week surfing the Internet, or holding conversations via e-mail.

◁ *Rollerblading was a new craze.*

Exercise

Children were said to spend too much time in front of computer or television screens. They weren't as fit as children used to be. But parents were often unwilling to let children play outside, or walk or ride bikes to school, because of the danger from high levels of traffic. Even so, many children did find places to enjoy the new craze, rollerblading, or ride their mountain bikes.

▷ Leonardo Di Caprio and Kate Winslet struggle to escape the sinking Titanic. Like many films in the 1990s, 'Titanic' made a second fortune for its producers when released on video.

A revival of cinema

The development of new multi-screen complexes helped cinema audiences to grow. However people often complained that only block-buster films, strongly 'hyped' by producers and distributors, were screened. *Jurassic Park*, directed by Steven Spielberg, and *Titanic*, directed by James Cameron, broke box-office records with their thrilling special effects. Together with Disney cartoons *Pocohontas* and *The Lion King*, they were soon released in video form for home-viewing, and led to lots of spin-off toys and merchandise.

One surprise hit was *Babe*, a film based on a children's story by Dick King-Smith. It used computerized imaging to make real animals appear to talk and act in a human way. *Forrest Gump*, starring Tom Hanks, used computer techniques to insert its hero into newsreel from recent history. Tom Hanks starred again in *Saving Private Ryan*, which was released in 1998. The film depicted with horrifying realism the Normandy landings that helped to end the Second World War. *Braveheart*, too, dealt with history and graphic battle scenes.

Profile

Nick Park

British animator Nick Park created Wallace and Grommit, whose adventures became Oscar-winning films. Wallace is a fussy Yorkshireman who makes weird inventions, and Grommit a comical dog with floppy ears. *Grand Day Out*, *The Wrong Trousers* and other films were created frame by frame, using plasticine figures and detailed sets made to scale. In 1996 Wallace and Grommit had a real adventure when Nick Park left the figures by mistake in a New York taxicab. Happily, they were returned unharmed.

Goodbye

River Phoenix,
actor;
Rudolf Nureyev,
ballet dancer;
Roald Dahl,
children's writer;
Satyajit Ray,
Indian film maker;
Ted Hughes, poet
(all died)

Hello

Leonardo Di Caprio;
Daniel Day Lewis;
Nicole Kidman;
Juliette Binoche;
Ewan McGregor;
Cate Blanchett
(actors)

n this case it was the story of William Wallace, a 13th-century Scottish hero who led a revolt against the English. The leading actor and director of *Braveheart*, Mel Gibson, became very popular among the Scots, who were seeking more independence from England in the 1990s.

In 1997 no fewer than nine Academy Awards (Oscars) went to *The English Patient*, a film based on a prize-winning novel. In 1999 a comedy *Shakespeare in Love* won seven Oscars.

As well as these high-budget movies, some British low-budget films were surprise big hits on both sides of the Atlantic. They were *Trainspotting*, *The Full Monty*, *Four Weddings and a Funeral* and *Mrs Brown*.

Roald Dahl's well-loved stories *The Witches*, *Matilda* and *James and the Giant Peach* were made into films, and so reached even larger audiences. In 1999 George Lucas released *The Phantom Menace*, a 'prequel' to his famous *Star Wars* trilogy, starring Ewan McGregor.

...Newsflash...

London, 27 May 1997. The new Globe Theatre opens tonight with a production of Shakespeare's play *Henry V*. It is built on the site of the original Globe Theatre which produced Shakespeare's plays 400 years ago, and in the exact same style. The theatre is circular, and open to the air. Those not seated under cover stand in the centre. When it rains, attendants give out plastic macs! Among the first to attend will be the prime minister's wife, Cherie Blair, and Hillary Clinton, accompanying her husband on his presidential visit to London.

Television

On television, *Barney the dinosaur* was popular with small children in the USA. British favourites were the *Teletubbies*, while older children loved Australian soap operas *Neighbours* and *Home and Away*. *Friends* and *Seinfeld* were two US comedy series which had fans everywhere. Oprah Winfrey was queen of 'confessional' programmes, where members of the public told about their real-life problems.

◁ *Children everywhere flocked to see American child star Macaulay Culkin in the 'Home Alone' movies.*

Date List

1990

11 February ▷ After the lifting of bans on the ANC in South Africa, Nelson Mandela is released after 27 years as a political prisoner.

31 March ▷ In London a huge demonstration against the Poll Tax turns into a full-scale riot. Young people in particular oppose Mrs Thatcher's new tax which they have never had to pay before.

5 July ▷ The Belgrade authorities dissolve Kosovo's parliament and sack its government after a Kosovan vote for independence. 1.7 million ethnic Albanians and 200,000 Serbs live in Kosovo. Serbs fear the majority want to join Kosovo to Albania.

2 August ▷ Iraqi forces invade Kuwait. The UN Security Council, including the USSR and China, condemns the invasion and agrees on a blockade or other military action should sanctions fail.

30 October ▷ At midnight, people in East and West Germany celebrate political reunification.

9 November ▷ Mary Robinson, an Independent in favour of civil and women's rights, becomes the first woman President of Ireland.

27 November ▷ Following the resignation of Margaret Thatcher, Conservative MPs elect John Major as their leader. He becomes prime minister.

1991

16 January ▷ USAF and allied planes attack Baghdad, Iraq, using laser-guided bombs and cruise missiles. Two days later, Iraq tries to widen the war, hitting Israel with Scud missiles.

24 February ▷ Allied tanks cross the Saudi Arabian border into Kuwait and Iraq. Thousands of Iraqi conscript soldiers are killed as they retreat. Three days later the Gulf War is over.

16 March ▷ The 'Birmingham Six' are released after 16 years in jail for a crime they did not commit. They had been beaten into signing confessions after an IRA pub bomb in Birmingham killed 21 people. This case was one of a number of miscarriages of justice involving Irish people which came to light in the 1990s.

1 August ▷ US President George Bush and Soviet President Mikhail Gorbachev sign the Strategic Arms Reduction Treaty (START), after nine years of negotiations. Both sides pledge to cut their nuclear arsenals by a third.

11 December ▷ The Maastricht Treaty is signed by leaders of countries in the European Union. Britain opts out of clauses on adopting the Social Chapter (which sets out basic rights for workers) and on a shared currency.

21 December ▷ The Soviet Union formally ceases to exist. Eleven former soviet republics, including Russia, form the Commonwealth of Independent States (CIS).

1992

10 April ▷ The day after a Conservative victory in Britain's general election, the IRA explodes a huge semtex bomb in the City of London.

20 April ▷ Expo '92, the first Universal Exposition for 22 years, opens in Spain.

29 April ▷ Riots break out in Los Angeles, after four white police officers accused of beating up black car driver Rodney King are found not guilty. The incident was videoed by a passer-by and widely broadcast. (In a second trial, a year later, two of the officers are found guilty.)

4 May ▷ The Canadian Inuit vote in favour of a limit to their territory in return for full citizenship and political rights. Their land is called Nunavut.

7 June ▷ Andrew Morton's book *Diana. Her True Story* reveals details of the unhappiness of the Princess of Wales, including her eating disorders.

15 August ▷ Photographs of starved prisoners held in Serbian camps in Bosnia are published in the world's press. The Red Cross confirms stories of the ill-treatment of Muslims and others.

4 October ▷ A Boeing 747 crashes into a block of flats in Amsterdam, killing hundreds. Local survivors suffer ill-health for years. In 1999 the authorities admit that the plane carried an Israeli cargo of materials to make nerve gas.

3 November ▷ In the US election, Bill Clinton (Democrat) receives 43 per cent of the vote, George Bush (Republican) 38 per cent, and Ross Perot (Independent) 19 per cent. Carol Moseley Braun is the first black woman elected to the Senate.

11 November ▷ After 17 years of fierce debate, the Synod (parliament) of the Church of England votes to allow women to be ordained as priests.

1993

15 January ▷ 130 countries sign a UNESCO chemical disarmament treaty. Possession and manufacture of weapons of mass destruction are forbidden. North Korea, Libya and Iraq do not sign.

19 April ▷ After a 51-day siege, federal agents storm the headquarters of the Branch Davidian cult, founded by David Koresh, in Waco, Texas. Cult leaders set fire to the property. Among those killed are 17 children.

July ▷ Abnormal rains in the Mississippi Basin cause the worst flooding in US history.

13 September ▷ Following secret talks in Oslo, Israel recognizes the PLO and the PLO renounces violence in favour of peaceful co-existence, in an agreement signed at the White House.

9 November ▷ The beautiful bridge at Mostar, in Bosnia, built in the 16th century by Sultan Suleiman, is destroyed by Croat shelling.

22 December ▷ The Australian parliament votes to restore to aborigines the rights to land taken from them by Europeans over 200 years ago. Mining companies oppose the decision.

1994

28 February ▷ Four Serb planes are shot down over Bosnia by NATO – its first offensive action.

6 April ▷ Civil war begins in Rwanda after President Habyarimana's plane is shot down.

29 April ▷ Polls open in South Africa's first democratic elections.

8 July ▷ Kim Il Sung, dictator of North Korea, dies. His son Kim Jong Il succeeds him. North Korea remains closed and secretive.

28 September ▷ Hundreds die when the roll-on, roll-off ferry *Estonia* sinks in the Baltic Sea. Experts say the design of ro-ro vessels is unsafe.

19 November ▷ Seven people share top prize in Britain's first national lottery.

1995

17 January ▷ An earthquake measuring 7.2 on the Richter scale devastates Kobe, Japan.

27 February ▷ London trading bank Barings collapses. Unregulated risk-taking on the Japanese stock exchange by trader Nick Leeson cost the bank millions of pounds.

3 March ▷ Dewayne Williams, who has five previous convictions for serious crimes, is sentenced to 25 years in jail for stealing a pizza. This follows President Clinton's new 'three strikes and you're out' policy, designed to impose tough sentences on persistent offenders.

19 April ▷ The Alfred P. Murrah building in Oklahoma City is bombed by white racists opposed to the US federal government.

7 May ▷ Celebrations and commemorations mark the 50th anniversary of the defeat of Nazi Germany and the end of the Second World War.

28 May ▷ An earthquake measuring 7.5 on the Richter scale destroys a town and damages an oil pipeline on Sakhalin island, far eastern Russia.

3 October▷ After a 9-month-long trial broadcast daily on TV, former American football star O. J. Simpson is found not guilty of the murder of his wife, Nicole Simpson, and her friend Ronald Goldman. Detective Mark Fuhrman has been shown to be racist, calling his evidence into doubt. A year later, Simpson is found responsible for the two deaths, in a civil trial.

1996

10 February▷ A blast at London's Canary Wharf breaks the IRA ceasefire of August 1994.

13 March▷ A crazed former scout leader, obsessed with guns, enters Dunblane primary school in Scotland and shoots dead 16 pupils, their teacher, and then himself.

25 March▷ Europe imposes a worldwide ban on the export of British beef. There is now proof of a link between BSE in cows and a new strain of fatal Creutzfeldt-Jakob disease in humans.

4 April▷ The so-called una-bomber is arrested in a remote part of Montana. For 17 years the former maths professor planted bombs in universities and computer stores.

28 August▷ The 15-year marriage of Prince Charles and Diana, Princess of Wales, ends in divorce. Charles denies that he intends to marry his long-term mistress Camilla Parker Bowles.

27 September▷ The Taleban introduce a fundamentalist Islamic state in Afghanistan.

1997

19 February▷ Deng Xiaoping, Chinese leader, dies aged 92. Jiang Zemin replaces him.

1 May▷ Tony Blair's new Labour win a landslide election victory in Britain. He has said his first three priorities are "Education, education, education."

31 August▷ Princess Diana and her friend Dodi Fayed are killed in a car crash in Paris.

5 September▷ Mother Theresa, founder of the Missionaries of Charity, dies in Calcutta.

20 September▷ Smog covers Indonesia and Malaysia after fires started in order to clear forest rage out of control in Borneo and Sumatra.

1998

January▷ Matt Drudge, who posts unchecked news and gossip on the Internet, publishes details of President Clinton's affair with Monica Lewinsky.

16 April▷ Pol Pot, leader of the Khmer Rouge, who ruled Cambodia with terror from 1975 to 1979, dies. He was never brought to justice.

28 May▷ Pakistan explodes five nuclear devices in retaliation for nuclear tests carried out by India.

1 September▷ A daily literacy hour is introduced into primary schools across Britain.

18 October▷ Former dictator General Pinochet is arrested in a London clinic. He led a US-backed military coup in Chile in 1973. Spanish judges want Britain to send him for trial for his part in the deaths and torture of thousands of people.

1999

24 February▷ Following a Public Inquiry into the murder of black teenager Stephen Lawrence in 1993, the MacPherson report finds the police to have been negligent and institutionally racist in not bringing charges against five white youths suspected of the murder.

24 March▷ NATO planes begin bombing Serbia. In the weeks that follow, Serbian paramilitaries intensify their attacks on ethnic Albanians in Kosovo, causing tens of thousands of refugees to flee to neighbouring countries.

2 June▷ The ANC wins South Africa's second general election. Thabo Mbeki becomes president. Nelson Mandela – widely acclaimed as man of the century – takes up retirement.

Glossary

aborigines

The original inhabitants of Australia, who were there when the Europeans arrived in the 1700s.

African National Congress (ANC)

A civil rights organization founded in 1912. Declared illegal by the South African government, which imprisoned its leaders or forced them into exile, the ANC continued to lead the struggle against apartheid. The ban on it was lifted in 1990, and it won the general elections held in 1994 and 1999.

AIDS

Acquired Immune Deficiency Syndrome, a fatal disease that first became known in the early '80s.

blockbuster

Name given to a movie made on a large-scale budget, often with extravagant locations and a large cast, with the intention of attracting big audiences and making big profits.

British Library

National library, previously based at the British Museum, which seeks to conserve and make available to scholars the widest possible collection of books published in English.

BSE

Bovine spongiform encephalopathy. Disease that attacks the brains of cows, causing them to lose coordination of movement, and then to die.

BST

Bovine somatotrophine. A synthetic hormone injected into cows to boost the quantity of milk they produce.

colonized

Settled and run by people from another country, for their profit and benefit. In the 18th and 19th centuries some European countries established empires made up of colonies all round the world. Some of these broke free through revolutionary war (for example, the USA, 1776) and some achieved independence through political agitation. Some remained as colonies into the 1990s (for instance, Hong Kong).

drag queen

Male entertainer dressed up in exaggerated female clothes.

El Niño

Spanish name, meaning 'the child', given to warming in the Pacific Ocean that occurs in certain years, affecting the world's climate in dramatic ways.

fundamentalist

Committed to a particular faith in an extreme or rigid way; especially allowing only a literal interpretation of religious texts, and no modernization of doctrine or forms of worship.

hereditary peer

Member of the British aristocracy, entitled to sit in the House of Lords (the upper chamber of parliament) as the first-born son, or otherwise heir, of a previously designated 'noble' family.

hyped

'Talked up' or promoted excessively.

Inuit

Once known as Eskimos, the Inuit are an ancient people living in Canada, Greenland and Alaska, whose traditional way of life revolved around hunting and fishing.

genetically modified (GM)

GM techniques enable scientists to alter the genetic material in a plant or animal, through manipulating cells in a laboratory, then introducing the cells back into the plant or animal. Some people are afraid this may bring harmful, and as yet unforeseen, consequences both to nature and to humans.

Good Friday Agreement

Agreement signed in 1998, which provided for the setting up of a power-sharing executive in Northern Ireland including Sinn Fein as well as Social Democrat and Unionist leaders. Cross-border authorities, overseen by the British and Irish governments, would cover certain areas of policy. Over time, paramilitary organizations must give up their weapons, and prisoners convicted of terrorist offences would be released.

landless peasants

Subsistence farmers whose land has been taken over by private individuals, companies or government agencies, often for deforestation or mining.

millennium

The year dates we use in the modern world are counted from the birth of Jesus Christ. Dates earlier than that work backwards, and are followed by the letters BC (Before Christ). So the year 2000 marks the passing of 2,000 years (two millennia), since the birth of Jesus. Because of the power of Christian societies in history, this dating system became accepted worldwide, even in non-Christian countries where it has no religious significance.

NATO

North Atlantic Treaty Organization. Military alliance involving the USA, Britain and various European nations, set up to guarantee the post-Second World War settlement in western Europe.

Nobel Prize

A highly prestigious prize awarded each year in Sweden for achievement on a world scale in the fields of Literature, Science and Peace.

no-fly zone

Area over which aircraft of a particular country are not allowed to fly. In the 1990s, no-fly zones were created in Iraq, to prevent Saddam Hussein's planes attacking Kurdish regions, and in Bosnia, to stop Serb air attacks. The zones were 'policed' by United Nations forces.

Palestine Liberation Organization (PLO)

The PLO was set up to represent Palestinian Arabs forced from their land when the Jewish state of Israel was established in 1948.

patented

New inventions are officially registered, and given a patent, to prevent them being copied or stolen, and to protect the commercial interest of the inventor. Others wishing to use the new invention must have the permission of the patent owner.

prequel

George Lucas subtitled his 1977 movie *Star Wars* as episode 4 in the story of a galaxy far, far away. Two sequels (follow-on movies) made up a trilogy. In 1999, his new film telling the story leading up to episode 4 was called a prequel.

Special Economic Zones

Areas of modern China where foreign investment and free enterprise are allowed. Internal borders separate these from the rest of China.

USSR

Union of Soviet Socialist Republics, a communist country founded out of the old Russian empire after the Bolshevik revolution of 1917.

New Words in the 1990s

New words or terms coined in the 1990s help give an idea of what was going on in the decade.

Many new words were concerned with computers. The **Internet** became a valuable source of information, and since so much new technology came from California, the word used to describe the activity of browsing through all this information came from the Californian West Coast too. But you didn't need a beach or breakers to **surf the net**.

Once **on line**, you could send and receive messages via **e-mail**, or be involved in **computer conferencing**. A fast-growing part of the Internet was the **World Wide Web** (**www**), on which people created **web sites** from which others could **down-load** information. **Search engines** were given unpretentious names such as 'dogpile', 'metacrawler' and 'yahoo'.

But you had to watch out if you stayed indoors using your computer all the time. You might be called a **mouse potato** (a new kind of couch potato) or even an **anorak**. At least you could claim to be **computer literate**; and you could keep a watch out for any **computer virus** hanging around in your system.

Schools banned them from the classroom, and people complained about their use in trains and restaurants, but it was hard to avoid that new instruction: '**Call me on my mobile!**' Mobile phones were everywhere. **Personal trainers** and political advisers, called **spin doctors**, could not operate without them.

No matter who you were, you should never leave young children **home alone**. You should try to be **politically correct** (**pc**) in what you said and did, especially as regards racism and sexism. But perhaps **girl power** had gone too far, with the way girls were outperforming boys in exams. Perhaps that's why there was so much **laddish** culture about – young men just doing their own thing? But women still said, when it came to promotion at work, that they seemed to hit an invisible barrier of prejudice that stopped them going further – a kind of **glass ceiling**.

Index